BEING ENERGY EFFICIENT

BY ROBIN TWIDDY

One SMALL STEP for kids, one giant leap towards SAVING the WORLD!

BookLife PUBLISHING

©2021
BookLife Publishing Ltd.
King's Lynn
Norfolk, PE30 4LS

Printed in Malta.

A catalogue record for this book is available from the British Library.

ISBN: 978-1-83927-848-8

Written by:
Robin Twiddy

Edited by:
Madeline Tyler

Designed by:
Drue Rintoul

PHOTO CREDITS

Images are courtesy of Shutterstock.com. With thanks to Getty Images, Thinkstock Photo and iStockphoto. 4&5 – Krakenimages.com, Hung Chung Chih, MOHAMED ABDULRAHEEM, Martin Bergsma, wonderisland, Ihor Bondarenko, NadyGinzburg. 6&7 – Mountain Brothers. 8&9 – Krakenimages.com, Alexey Seafarer, Kenneth Keifer, Maximillian cabinet. 10&11 – Krakenimages.com, Andrey_Popov, Quang nguyen vinh, Richard Nantais, engel.ac. 12&13 – Krakenimages.com, Breadmaker, Joeri Mostmans, michaeljung, Iryna Kuznetsova. 14&15 – Krakenimages.com, Mohammad Fahmi Abu Bakar, Wirestock Creators, ShutterLibrary, dencg, Ivan Production, ApoGapo, oksana2010. 16&17 – Maxx-Studio, LightField Studios, Hananeko_Studio, rikur B. 18&19 – FrameStockFootages, montira areepongthum, Asier Romero, Leszek Glasner, FamVeld. 20&21 – Krakenimages.com, Prostock-studio, MODMOD, Chalermchai Chamnanyon, Prostock-studio, VladKK, Lucian Coman, mr.kriangsak kitisak. 22&23 – Daboost. 24&25 – Mike_shots, Lordn, Sean Pavone, Pixel-Shot, smile23, PicMy, Andrey_Popov, Fotokostic, Linagagaga, Mark Nazh, Africa Studio, ANURAK PONGPATIMET, Mostovyi Sergii Igorevich, wavebreakmedia. 26&27 – Krakenimages.com, Monkey Business Images, Inside Creative House, Fuss Sergey. 28&29 – Dmytro Zinkevych, adriaticfoto. 30 – Krakenimages.com.

CONTENTS

Words that look like this are explained in the glossary on page 31.

You can (help) Save the World

The world is in trouble and it needs your help! It needs everyone's help. No one can save the world on their own, but together we can make a change. Our planet is facing many challenges, and lots of these are because of humans. The climate crisis is a big problem. We can see how humans have made it worse by looking at changes in the weather, the oceans and the air we breathe.

ROBIN TWIDDY PRESENTS:

THE SMALL STEPS REVOLUTIONARIES

These are the Small Steps Revolutionaries. They are changing the world one step at a time. Whether it's being energy efficient or learning how to compost, eating locally or living zero waste, recycling or using water wisely, no problem is too big or too small for this band of heroes. By the time you finish this book you too will be a member of the Small Steps Revolution. Strap in, recruit – it's time to save the world!

Grow Your Knowledge

The first step to becoming a Small Steps Revolutionary is growing your knowledge. This means learning as much as you can about the change you want to see. There are lots of ways to grow your knowledge. Here are some places to get started.

Learn from others – do you know anyone who is already energy efficient? Ask them about it.

Visit the library – ask the librarian to help you find books about the environment.

"Knowledge is power – arm yourself!"

"The end of all knowledge should be service to others."
– Cesar Chavez

Cesar Chavez was a Mexican American civil rights activist who worked on making things fairer for workers.

"Those who do not learn from history are doomed to repeat it!"

Simone de Beauvoir was a French writer who thought a lot about how we live our lives, and was part of the fight for equality for women.

"Change your life today. Don't gamble on the future, act now, without delay."
– Simone de Beauvoir

Research online – there are lots of great websites about being energy efficient.

SMALL STEP: GROW YOUR KNOWLEDGE!

Knowledge is important but make sure that the information you look at is accurate. A good way to do that is to see who else agrees, writes or talks about the same information. Has it come from a reliable place or person?

Saving the World One Switch at a Time

Kim is a **Small Steps Revolutionary**. Being a **Small Steps Revolutionary** means making small changes in your own life to help make a change around the world and inspire others to do the same.

I am always thinking about how to be **energy efficient**. It is just one small thing we can all do to help the environment. Whatever I am doing, I try to see if I can only use what I need.

I became a **Small Steps Revolutionary** so that I could do my part to help spread this important message. In this book, me and my friends will show you ways that you can take Small Steps towards saving the world by becoming more **energy efficient**.

THE HIDDEN COST

The climate crisis is one of the greatest threats to the world and is one of the main reasons that the **Small Steps Revolution** was started. But what is it, and what is causing it?

CLIMATE CHANGE

The atmosphere is something that goes around our planet. It is made up of lots of different gases. These gases have lots of jobs that keep our planet healthy, but one of these jobs is controlling how much heat escapes from our planet into space. If there is a change in how much of each gas is in the atmosphere, it can affect the temperature and weather on Earth. We call this climate change.

Climate means the usual or normal weather and temperature of a place.

Why Be Energy Efficient?

Do you ever think about where the energy that powers your TV, tablets, computers and even your lights comes from?

The energy we use to power things such as our lights and TVs is called electricity. Most of our electricity comes from big power plants that burn fossil fuels. Fossil fuels are made from very old plants and animals that died millions of years ago. Burning fossil fuels helps us make electricity, but it also makes CO_2. CO_2 is one of the gases that causes climate change.

LIMITED RESOURCES

The other problem with fossil fuels is that they will run out. It takes millions of years for them to be made naturally. This means that one day there will be none left. We should use as many types of renewable energy as we can.

Solar panels collect energy from the Sun. This is called solar energy.

Wind turbines use the power of the wind to make electricity.

This dam at a hydroelectric plant uses hydro energy to make electricity.

Changing Habits

Being a Small Steps Revolutionary means being aware of the little things – the things we do every day without even noticing. To make a big difference, we need to take some Small Steps. Here are some that you can take in your own home.

A LITTLE LIGHT CAN LEAD TO BIG WASTE

When you leave a room, do you always turn the lights off? Millions of people don't. Together, all those lights waste a huge amount of energy and make loads of CO_2.

Make it a habit to turn the lights off when you leave a room!

TURN OFF THAT TV

When you aren't watching the TV, don't leave it on – turn it off at the wall.

Don't forget your games console! If you need to stop for dinner, save your game and turn it off – don't just leave it on pause!

SAVE YOUR GAME TO SAVE THE PLANET!

FAST AT THE FRIDGE

Make up your mind about what you want from the fridge before you open the door. All the time that the fridge is open, it is using extra power. That means extra CO_2 is being released into the atmosphere.

SMALL STEPS:

- SWITCH OFF LIGHTS
- TURN GADGETS OFF AT THE WALL
- DON'T LEAVE THE FRIDGE OPEN

Standby for Destruction

GIVE ME CONVENIENCE AT ANY COST

Convenience is when something is really helpful, easy and usually doesn't need much effort. However, convenience comes at a cost. Most TVs have a standby mode. When things are on standby, it may seem like they are off, but they are still using power.

Any device that has a little light or digital clock on after you have turned it off is still using power.

TURN IT OFF AT THE WALL

One **Small Step** that we can take is to turn off our electrical <u>appliances</u> at the wall. Hunt around your house for things that use standby mode or use power when they are not in use.

UNDERCOVER POWER-DRAINING APPLIANCES

ROUTER AND MODEM

We can access the internet instantly, but who is using the internet when everyone in the house is asleep?

STEREOS, MICROWAVES AND ANYTHING WITH A DIGITAL CLOCK

It is handy to know the time, but how many digital clocks do we need? Turn them off.

48"
42"

SET TOP BOX

The ***set top box*** *is always ready to play TV programmes, but it is also always using power.*

TELEVISION

A TV on standby is always ready to play your favourite shows, but it is also always using power.

Think about whether you need these things being powered all the time. If you can turn a few of these off when they are not in use then that will be one **Small Step** towards being **energy efficient**.

SMALL STEP:
LEARN WHICH APPLIANCES USE ENERGY WHEN SWITCHED OFF

A Little Elbow Grease

Lots of the machines we have in our homes are there to make jobs around the house easier. They save us a lot of time, but we can do without some of them.

The legion of convenient doom!

YOU ARE THE DISHWASHER

Do you have a dishwasher in your house? Once a week, try washing your dishes by hand. You will find that it doesn't take long, and it is one Small Step towards being energy efficient.

Washing dishes together with your family can be really fun.

NOW YOU'RE COOKING WITHOUT GAS (OR ELECTRICITY)

Another **Small Step** you can take is having one or two meals a week that don't need to be cooked. Talk to your adults and see if you can help prepare the meal.

*The more fun a **Small Step** is, the more likely you are to do it again.*

POWERED BY THE ELEMENTS

Help your adults to make energy efficient choices. Try hanging your wet washing outside on a clothesline or inside on an airer. This is better than using a tumble dryer.

Tumble dryers use a lot of energy.

SMALL STEP: DO SOME CHORES BY HAND

Small Changes

Being energy efficient can be hard when the things you like doing use electricity, such as watching TV, playing computer games or playing electric instruments.

*Being a **Small Steps Revolutionary** is about making small changes. You don't need to give up doing all the things you like that use electricity – just try to do some activities you enjoy that use less electricity.*

Remember, it is about making **Small Steps** and keeping to them. Try lots of new energy efficient hobbies. I am sure you will find something you love.

ALL SORTS OF WAYS TO PLAY

Instead of playing online games, try card and board games with your friends and family. It is fun to sit around the table playing board games together!

GET CRAFTY

Arts and crafts are a brilliant way to spend your time – you could make some art to tell other people about the **Small Steps Revolution.**

Get outside and get some exercise. You could play sports with your friends or take up running. Exercise isn't just a great way to pass the time without using electricity – it is good for you too!

SMALL STEP: FIND SOME HOBBIES THAT DON'T USE ELECTRICITY

Saving Water

Did you know that using water in your house uses power too? My friend Ron is an expert at **Being Wise with Water.**

Hi, I am Ron and I'm here to tell you about why wasting water is bad for the environment. Firstly, it uses power to run the water pumps in your house, and secondly the water that comes through our taps comes from natural **water sources** that can be damaged if too much water is taken from them before they can be refilled.

So, let's **Get Wise with Water** around the house.

Fix dripping taps

A dripping tap can lose roughly 180 litres of water a day!

Keep a bottle of water in the fridge for when you want cold water. This will save you from running the tap until it is cold enough.

Old cups of water can be used to feed plants instead of being poured down the sink.

Only a small amount of the water in the world is fresh water, and the rest is salt water like you find in the sea. We need to look after that fresh water because we need it to drink, bathe, clean and so much more.

SMALL STEPS:

- USE OLD WATER TO FEED PLANTS
- USE REFRIGERATED WATER INSTEAD OF RUNNING A TAP UNTIL COLD
- FIX DRIPPING TAPS

*To learn more about **Being Wise with Water**, check out Ron's book.*

The Efficiency Challenge

It is time to see how energy efficient you have become. You will need a journal, or somewhere you can write down your energy-saving efforts.

THE ENERGY YOU USE

Keep track of any activities you do that use energy and write about them in your journal. How long did you spend watching TV or listening to music? How long did you play on your games console for?

07:00 AM – 30 MINUTES WATCHING TV WHILST EATING BREAKFAST

07:30 AM – WENT ON MY GAMES CONSOLE

07:40 AM – PLAYING MUSIC ON MY PHONE WHILST GETTING DRESSED

Use these notes about how much energy you have used to try and use less next week.

ENERGY-SAVING ACTIVITIES

Don't just record when you are using energy, make sure you record all the times you save energy, too. Write down every time you choose an activity that doesn't use energy, and every time you manage to cut down your energy use. So, if you choose to play outside rather than on the computer, write it down.

07:00 AM – 30 MINUTES WATCHING TV WHILST EATING BREAKFAST
(COULD READ OR TALK TO MY FAMILY INSTEAD)

07:30 AM – PLAYED A QUICK GAME OF CARDS WITH MY SISTER

07:40 AM – PLAYING MUSIC ON MY PHONE WHILST GETTING DRESSED (DOESN'T TAKE LONG TO GET DRESSED – I DON'T NEED MUSIC ON YET)

HOW I HAVE SAVED ENERGY

- TURNED TV OFF AT THE SOCKET
- PLAYED OUTSIDE INSTEAD OF ON MY PHONE
- UNPLUGGED MY PHONE CHARGER BETWEEN CHARGES

SMALL STEP: KEEP AN ENERGY JOURNAL

Keeping track of your successes is a great way to stay motivated. Seeing how much energy you are saving will keep you focused. Recruit an adult to help you share your **Small Step Successes** online with **#smallstepsrevolution**

Small Steps in Action

Small Steps add up to big changes. Keep an eye on the power bar. These **Small Steps Revolutionaries** are saving energy, becoming more energy efficient and saving the world.

The dishwasher uses lots of energy – either wait until you can fill it to make the most of that power or...

... wash the dishes by hand!

Clothes dryers use lots of power to do something that can be done for free.

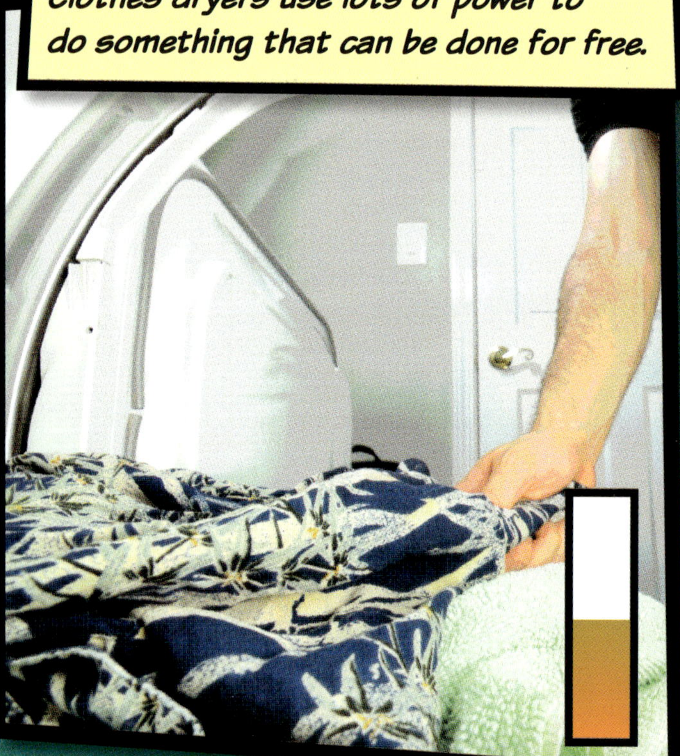

That's it – hang your washing up inside or outside to save the day.

Computer games are really fun, but so are...
... board games.
There is lots to watch on TV, but it is better for the planet and for you to...
... get outside and play some sport.
Don't turn the heat up when it gets cold...
... try wrapping up warm first.
If you can't see in the daytime, don't switch the lights on...
... open the curtains.
Getting about by car is fine, but if you don't need to go far...
... hop on your bike and save some power!

Becoming a Champion of Change

Being a Small Steps Revolutionary is more than just taking Small Steps yourself – it also means being a champion of change. We can do this by showing others the steps we are taking and sharing our passion for protecting the planet.

RAISING AWARENESS

There are lots of ways that you can raise awareness as a Small Steps Revolutionary. Some revolutionaries use social media to share their message. Recruit an adult to help you manage an account. Remember not to use social media without an adult you trust.

Remember, computers use power, so don't spend too long on there.

If you are creative, you could decorate your bag or make a t-shirt with messages that encourage people to be energy efficient.

Be the change you want to see.

*Look for places that you can make a change. Are there any **Small Steps** that could help your school to become more energy efficient? Talk to a teacher and see if you can help them to make a change.*

***Small Steps Revolutionaries** are proud to make a change!*

*Share your successes with the hashtag **#smallstepsrevolution***

Energy-saving light bulbs use less energy to make the same light as normal bulbs.

Remember, some people might not have met anyone making the changes you are making, so be nice when you talk about being energy efficient. People are more likely to try to make a change themselves if you are helpful instead of being mean to them – this is the **Small Steps** way!

SMALL STEPS: SHARE YOUR SUCCESSES

Ethical Living

Being energy efficient is only one part of the Small Steps Revolution, so what does it mean to be a Small Steps Revolutionary? It means living ethically – living the best life you can. To live ethically you need to think about the effect your actions have on the world around you.

MAKING THE CHANGE

Making the change to being energy efficient is not easy and won't happen overnight. Remember the golden rule: Small Steps Lead to Big Change. Focus on making small changes that you can keep to every day; every small step will take you closer to being energy efficient.

THE FIVE Rs

A good way to guide your actions as a Small Steps Revolutionary is to live by the 5 Rs. They are:

REFUSE – BEFORE YOU BUY SOMETHING, THINK HARD ABOUT WHETHER YOU NEED IT OR NOT. IF YOU DON'T, THEN REFUSE TO BUY OR ACCEPT IT.

REDUCE – SOME THINGS YOU WILL NOT BE ABLE TO REFUSE, BUT YOU CAN USE LESS. THIS WILL MEAN YOU CREATE LESS WASTE.

REUSE – BEFORE YOU THROW SOMETHING AWAY, THINK ABOUT WHETHER THAT THING CAN BE USED AGAIN. ONLY REPLACE SOMETHING IF IT CAN'T BE USED AGAIN.

REPURPOSE – THIS IS ANOTHER WAY OF SAYING UPCYCLE. IF YOU CAN, FIND A NEW WAY TO USE SOMETHING INSTEAD OF THROWING IT AWAY.

RECYCLE – IF YOU CAN'T DO ANY OF THESE THINGS THEN YOU SHOULD TRY TO RECYCLE. MAKE SURE THAT WHAT YOU PUT INTO YOUR RECYCLING BIN CAN BE RECYCLED BY YOUR LOCAL RECYCLING CENTRE.

Manifesto

THE BEING ENERGY EFFICIENT MANIFESTO

- SWITCH OFF LIGHTS
- TURN APPLIANCES OFF AT THE WALL
- DON'T LEAVE THE FRIDGE OPEN
- GROW YOUR KNOWLEDGE
- LEARN WHICH APPLIANCES USE ENERGY WHEN SWITCHED OFF
- DO SOME CHORES BY HAND
- FIND SOME HOBBIES THAT DON'T USE ENERGY
- USE OLD WATER TO FEED PLANTS
- USE REFRIGERATED WATER INSTEAD OF RUNNING A TAP UNTIL COLD
- FIX DRIPPING TAPS
- KEEP AN ENERGY JOURNAL
- SPREAD THE MESSAGE
- USE THE FIVE RS

You are now a full member of the **Small Steps Revolution**. Keep on taking small, sustainable steps, spreading the word and inspiring others to do the same. Together we can and will **Save the World**.

Glossary

APPLIANCES	electrical items used to carry out a job or task
CIVIL RIGHTS ACTIVIST	someone who fights for other people's rights
CLIMATE CRISIS	serious problems being caused by changes to the world's weather, caused by humans and the release of greenhouse gases into the environment
CREATIVE	having an ability to make new things or think of new ideas
ENERGY	the power to do something
ENVIRONMENT	all the things that make up the natural world
EQUALITY	having the same, fair treatment and rights as other people
FRESH WATER	clean, saltless water that is found in nature
RECRUIT	to bring a member into a group
RELIABLE	can be trusted
RENEWABLE	can be replaced
SALT WATER	natural water with a high level of salt, such as the sea
SET TOP BOX	an electrical item that receives television stations
SOCIAL MEDIA	websites and apps that let users create and share things, as well as talk with each other
SUSTAINABLE	able to be used without damaging future generations
THREATS	things that could cause trouble or harm
UPCYCLED	taking something old and used and turning it into something brand new and better
WATER SOURCES	places that water naturally comes from

Index